Words with Meaning

Abby Perratt

Presentation by *BookLeaf Publishing*

Web: www.bookleafpub.com

E-mail: info@bookleafpub.com

ISBN: 9789358316063

First edition 2023

This book is dedicated to a life I have lived and all those in it. If you really know me you'll know what's for you. I look forward to facing the rest of it with you.

....and a special thanks to the one who lent me the money to do it!

ACKNOWLEDGEMENT

Poetry is an art and therefore is in the eyes of the reader. Take from this what you will but all material is entirely my own.

My life, my pets, my friends and most importantly my choices.

PREFACE

Everyone walks a different path, there are so many variations of life. What is important to some is of no concern to others, what is problematic or devastating to some is not a worry to others. The point is that you can't judge based on only your own experience, the key to life is trying to maintain an open mind and open attitude. Remember others don't see the world the same as you. All we can do is our best, just be kind and don't be cruel.

This book of poetry aims to make the reader take a moment to consider something they have not considered before. Perhaps re-looking at an occasion or incident and imagine a different perspective, maybe look at someone in your life a little differently or even just decide to take a walk and see some things you've never taken the time to really acknowledge before. Perhaps if you need, it will help you feel just a little bit lighter about what is on the horizon. We all have the strength, it's just if we decide to use it.

Forest Of Ash

The spirits they gather in the forests of ash
Energies of sorts rumble and clash
Bleak is the morning that hangs on the dawn
Twisted and broken the sweet little fawn
Clutching the safe place before the sun comes
Beasties be darting, they scatter and run
Seen and not this feeling repent
To behold the meaning of all moral spent
Creeping are the trees over the ground
Bewitching it seems the air all around
Fragile if feels each thing to touch
Potently looming the air is too much
Here in the forest were true mystic lies
Time is but nothing and all judgement dies
Stark in the centre, a pool of despair
Where the willing can come and release the care
The forest will have you, for all that your worth
Humility is nothing if you do not walk the earth
Here in this place you can fully discover
How to walk one path and also another
Just take the step toward the unknown
And look for the signs there to be shown
Wait for the magic, take time to ponder
At nightfall the forest will
take hold of great wonder.

The battle of old

These blood stained clothes
are cold and wet
The dripping sound could louder
get
Feeling the burn down my skin
An eternity battle never to win
Seeing of the flesh is a comfort to know
I'm in control there's room to grow
Feelings so cold it freezes my heart
Numb and empty right from the start
A desperate emotion yet calm at the thought
Up in this web I'm already caught
This is my prison, in which I am kept
Forever it seems I cannot have slept
Demons they spill right out of this
Black are the figures that withhold bliss
All that's there is white noise and static
Mind a blur understanding erratic
Mental is the torture to endure
Slow is the sting forevermore
Alone in the dark trying to focus
Submerged away from the hocus pocus
Beasties living trying to breath
This part is the test from which I want to be freed.

The Road

On this road, don't know where it's going
Left for dead no chances of slowing
In the meek of the night the thoughts go round
An ever playing narrative echoes the sound

Based upon the noises left inside my head
I know I've pretty much lost it, just keeping the demons fed

To lose yourself is to lose it all
All it takes is one trip and fall
From which you don't regain
And your heart, it begins to drain

The cold it consumes, and the sorrow it takes a hold
Leaving you worthless cause that's all you've ever been told

Staring up at the night sky
Pleading with the world, asking why
But the blackness does not hold the answers
This fight is internal, it's all about your candor
To look in is to find your strength
To know yourself, is to win

On The Inside

My mind is a cage
It's filling with rage
With this sin from within
My morals wear thin
This world it feels cold
And my heart cannot hold
Onto a thing
Without a steel ring
Pulling heavy on my neck
But never to check
If I am still breathing
Or just about leaving
This world all behind
But only to find
I'm still pushing on
Never to be gone
The fights there are many
With no luck of a penny
Come my way no more
For this I am sure
The lessons are hard
With never a shard
Of hope in this sea
Of total misery
The pressure too much
I can't feel the touch
Of my own bare soles
Upon hot burning coals
This body is numb
To the dull constant hum
Of pain in this life
So I look to the knife

To take back control
Of the life as a whole
Find comfort to see
That I can still bleed
If the world keeps on turning
I will keep yearning
For better for me
And release, from my own insanity.

The End

To feel the daze descend
It's like a sign of the end
I struggle to stay sober
Knowing that it's over
To feel the heavy hand
Of guilt come down to land
These feelings that I know
Are cold and go to show
Just how sad it is
This is how bad it is
To repeat a notion
Of complete back motion
Seeming to go round
Leading nowhere but the ground
For this is going the wrong way
No longer just a game to play
This is indeed real time
And it's down to me to get mine
No one else will be there
To share in the same care
Or to tell me how it's done
Before I'm caught on the run.

Life

Always give a thought
To what you have been taught
Cause time doesn't allow for mistakes
Ever at the ready
Remain calm and steady
Cause this game's all about the high stakes.

Out Of Place

My head cannot fathom
This nightmare I'm having
The nauseas is too much
I can't feel the touch
Of your hand on my skin
It's wearing too thin
My breaths running out
I just need to shout
To the world if its listening
I'm just about missing
Every point that there is
To this life and its glitz
I'm rolling along
But it all feels wrong
When did it change
I'm feeling deranged
It just doesn't fit
But I'm taking the hit
For now it still matters
Until it's all shattered
The choices I make
Are totally fake
But one day I'll know
And then it will be so.

Face Value

I'm drowning, treading water, just trying to stay afloat
The answers hazy, hard to find, it's time to grab a coat
The weather's turning, the rain is starting to pour
Always looking for the next step, to take me through the
door
Into a new life, one that begins to grow
Into something truly beautiful to finally let me show
Just what I am made of, there's so much to see
I've got a lot to give and I'm willing to pay the fee
There are whispers in the darkness, look to the sky above
See it in the shine of the stars, the future looks full of love
Time is short and it is precious, it's not too late to change
If there's strength enough to make it through, nothing's out
of range
Always shoot for the best, but hold good morals high
Stand fast in those positive friendships and hold the hurtful
lies
Show kindness to a stranger, share a helping hand
These small kind actions will help the point to land
There's more to me than meets the eye
I'm just a little bit shy.

Endless

Endless is the notion of never ending grey
Nothing in this life ever seems to pay
Buried beneath this great crushing weight
I hold on for dear life to discover my fate
If one day or another I decide to give up
Nothing awaits me, all doors remain shut

Endless in the notion never to know
If the future holds better or just more of this low
It feels like a slow death, no greater shame
Than the loneliness of this life, alone in the rain
The blackness surrounds, the air it is cold
My soul it feels empty, nothing to hold

Endless is the notion that good won't prevail
This life is tormented, destined to derail
The struggle is real I just try to find
The strength if enough to not lose my mind
These days are a chance to see if the toil
Wins me the battle or leads me to the soil.

Moving

Heavy is the heart this night
Weary body cannot take the fight
Solemn is the face of true
Weeping bare thoughts but a few
This silence deafens the world in all
Utter darkness begins the fall
Of future and past
This disdain to last
Eternity and a minute
To push me to my limits
For better or worse
To lift this curse
I must conquer
Myself no longer
For this matter is bigger
Than my mind can figure
Heavy it is to wear the chains
More even it is to carry the pains
To look for the brightness
To know how to fight this
Beginnings anew
Will come with a few
Sacrifices and change
To broaden the range
Of hope and embrace
To win this great race.

Ready Steady, You're Already Gone

Wherever you go
You'll continue to know
Everything keeps growing
And time keeps going
One foot then the next
Don't feel vexed
Lives are all short
So don't get caught
Up in the puzzle
Continue to guzzle
See everything
Just take it all in
The world is charging
No need to be starving
Of emotional stuff
It's always tough
But with strong of will
There's no time to kill
It's all already underway.

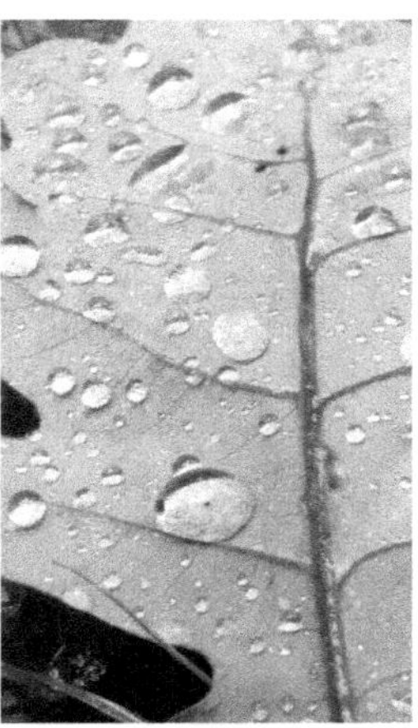

You've Just Got To See

This life laid out before you
with all its twists
and turns

Everyone's is different,
the good and the hurt

You never know the distance, nor what lies ahead
Just keep looking for those things to keep your soul fed

Find the warm in the sunshine, the breath in the air
Keep your eyes open, you never know what's there

The beauty is around you, you've just got to see
Even on the dark days, its power holds the key

It's not unlike what you've seen before
But maybe this time you'll appreciate it more

Keep your mind open, the world isn't fair
But little by little you'll find yourself there

To share a smile with
someone you see
Pass on a good
gesture and let all
just be

All the good things that make it our world
Will always be there to let you feel heard
Look for the signs, no matter how small
There will always be something, that's an
absolute rule!

Time

It's ever changing but a constant in life
It's always on the move and often the strife
Of many people's days and even their nights
It's with you always, try as you might
It comes with the best things, as well of the worst
It's obvious to us all and brings with it a thirst
To get the very most out of every little bit
We must focus on each moment and find the best fit
On how we wish to walk the line
And spend each second of our time
Call it a moment or even a price
Sometimes it's negative sometimes it's nice
You can't control it so don't even try
Just take it as it comes and enjoy the high.

Push Me

Willing to be tested
But won't let be bested
The shadows weigh heavy
On these shoulders they levy
The demons are thriving
Souls barely surviving
Dreaming of numbness
Scorning the dumbness
The best or the worst
You'll have to take me in a hearse
With heavy hearts of sorrow
For the thoughts of tomorrow
The brightness won't come
Follow the sound of the drum
Til no more is sought
And the dreams are all bought
And left is the potion
That brings forth the notion
That nothing is forever
And together will be never
Alone in the darkness
Screaming the starkness
Of bare hopes and broken thoughts
All quite something of sad sorts.

Never Say Never

With some wind and a feather
Never say never
The world just might have something in store
Always be hopeful
Never stay woeful
Cause this time it just might be yours.

A Walk Through The Woods

A walk through the woods you're taking a ponder
Being in nature just makes you wonder
About all of the things from the bug to the tree
The sounds and the sights, there's so much to see
The sing of the songbirds all around you
The snap of the sticks under your shoe
The odd falling acorn, and leaves on the ground
A scampering squirrel collecting nuts he has found
The crystal clear stream runs down the hillside
Take in the beauty, keep your mind open wide
The smells of a new day circle your nose
The calls of the buzzards help ease your woes
The fog hangs heavy throughout the valley
The insects of the forest begin to dally
And then within a short time
The sun it will begin to shine
And the woods are alive, with its new dawn day surprise.

Everyday

To that friend who's no longer there
I hope you knew how much I care
I live your honour everyday
And try not to lose sight of the way
I'll hold you close in my heart forever
As you watch over me and every endeavour

Storm

Hear the skies rumble
Far distant grumble
The storm is approaching
Ever encroaching
The air hangs thick
You've just got to pick
Which way to run
Into the hum
Of the electricity air
Without even a care
Or away from the threat
If only to get
Another dry second
Before being beckoned
To look to the sky
At a million silent cries
As the raindrops are falling
The clouds are all balling
A dark menace surrounds
The thunder it hounds
The wind she rips
Right through the grips
Of all things now swirling
Wrestling and hurling
The sky is now screaming
The strong trees leaning
The water it pours
The air it roars
The lightning is cracking
The wind is smacking
Right in your face
To give you a taste

Of things elemental
The harsh and the gentle
The storm is hear
But hold your fear.

You & Me

You are the passion of my heart
I hope we never have to part
Your the essence of my life
I want to make you my wife
Forever might seem a long time
But I will always help you shine
The path with you is so much brighter
And with each day our bond grows tighter

One Good Thing

If this life is a mission
Maybe stop and listen
To the world and its calling
Before you start falling
Into its trap
You must find the map
To a better tomorrow
Away from the sorrow
And climb to the top
Never to stop
Just keep on living
Try selflessly giving
To someone in need
Your soul will be freed
Thanks will shine on you
Your heart will be true
The good ripple grows
And the kindness it goes
Into the sea
Of complete positivity
One day it will come
Just like the sun
To repay your thought
In goodness of sort
And the world she goes on
Trying to balance the wrong.

I try

You're there for me always
I try not to take you for granted
You stand by me everytime
I try to make you proud

You lift me up when I am down
I try to never stumble
You keep me grounded when I feel I'm drowning
I try to stay on course

You hear me when I'm talking
I try to speak up
You think of me in times of need
I try to do it right

You make my life a better place
I try to live it to the most
I give to you a piece of my heart
So try to keep it safe.

This Amazing Place

What a stunning place, this world in which we live
Every small drop of it has something else to give
For those of you who know me it may not surprise
To hear me say such things and be someone who tries
To give it the utmost and look for the good
The amazing and spectacular, and that not understood
The smallest of details even the bark of a tree
The process of freezing, the wings of a bee
It's all around us, the beauty in the rain
Or the sound of thunder, it's all knowledge to gain
From the creation of glaciers to how ants make a home
How spiders make webs, that stuff they call sea foam
It amazing to think about how the world grows
And the bright little fireflies and their beautiful light shows
The shape of a snowflake or how fish swim in schools
Even the small things that live in rock pools
These things are incredible, those patterns in nature
As your mind comprehends these things are even greater
The makeup of the human eye or the sound of a night lark
This stuff blows my mind like how mould grows in the
dark
You'd think some things just couldn't be real
But lo and behold it's the real deal.

Gone But Never Without

25

To the pets that have passed I just want to say
Your memories are cherished each and every day
I give you my love even still now
Forever and always, I make it a vow
Your life was a blessing, I'm so lucky to have had
For those who choose not to, I think that you're mad!
They gave so much love, I couldn't have managed without
Living life and loving, is what it's all about.

Before Now And Always

The wind on the morrow
Shall continue to follow
The cloud of the past
Ever to last
Before now and always
It's all just a haze
When it comes to the end
We all off and send
Ourselves right into the ground.

My Dog

My love for you is like no other
Nothing can compare, not even my mother!
She'll hate that I said that
And so will my cat
But right by my side
Is where you'll be sat
Forever my friend, always my dog
My four legged sweetheart, a total attention hog
You slobber on me daily and scratch me with your claws
But I'll always love your yoda face and your little white
paws
You leave fluff on my sheets and mud in my car
But your hugs are the best and your bandana is the cutest
by far.
Your loyal to the bone, and you love your tennis ball
You're my first dog and best, even when you're a fool.

To My Friend

I'll hold you in my heart forever, a special place for you to
stay
You're in my mind from day to day, there to help me along
the way

You're always there to hear me, even if it's just to listen
You always share perspective that seems to make things
glisten

I trust in your judgement all of the time
I hear truth from you always, to keep me in line

I love your approach to life, and all things that matter
The best thing for me is when we just sit and natter

Your hugs are the best, as a person you are stunning
I'll always be there for you, we'll just keep on running

Through life side by side til' we get to the top
Nothing can stop us, no surely not!

Your soul is a good one and I'll never let you forget
Your being is priceless, so hold no regrets

You should have only joy, cause you deserve nothing less
You're my best friend always, no need to guess

I'll love you forever, in my heart you are there
All through life and everything, with you I will share :)

Potentially

Take a breath, hold it tight
Take a leap, right into flight
The world is before you
And nothing can stop you
From giving it your best shot
Why the heck not
It's amazing to me
If you actually try to see
All that is in you, is surprisingly more
Than what you first thought
The things you can do
With your mind in right view
Is utterly insane
There is so much to gain
It's not for the takers
It's there for the makers
Of their own dream
It's starting to seem
A desperate situation
To no alleviation
You must just try
For without it's all a lie
And you will never know
If you're able to grow.

Mixed messages

It's burning, I'm turning
Mostly concerning
Myself with all things
Til the new bell rings
And you're all astounded
For I'm higher grounded
Than ever did you think
In only a blink
I work my magic
And suddenly the tragic
Is a faint distant cry
From what is a lie
Until you remember
That inside ember
Has fire in it still
Just enough to fill
The lives of the loved
And those up above
And suddenly it's here
Pushing back the fear
To let it soak in
Will lead to the win.

Every Moment

When your life looks like it's about to derail
Learn from the mistakes, it's the best way to fail
You never know what's coming, that's what makes the
game
But anything other than your best would be an awful shame
Pick yourself up and brush yourself off
Cause you don't know how long you've really got
It's not a race to the finish but it's about how you play
Making every moment matter each single day.

Voices

You can tell that I'm falling
Right into the calling
Out of my heart
It was right from the start
I should have just listened
To my life's ongoing mission
To give myself over
Like the white cliffs of Dover
To bare it all out
Stand tall and shout
Cause it's never the end
If there's still strength to send
Away all the troubles
If they're only to double
The future is hazy
It doesn't make you lazy
To feel that feeling
That leaves your heart reeling
It's only what your told
It'll never get old
But those people won't help you
There's not but a few
It's about all our choices
We've just got to find our voices.

Hindsight

If only I'd known this before
I wouldn't keep thinking of it more
With hindsight upon me
I down tool and run free
Cause there just isn't the need to be scared.

Lost but not forgotten

To the parents that look down on us now
Please know, it's your guidance we know how
We know how to live
We know how to love
But each and everyday you are missed
It's a trouble without you
But at least you've got a good view
As you watch over our lifetime
And shine down on us each night time.

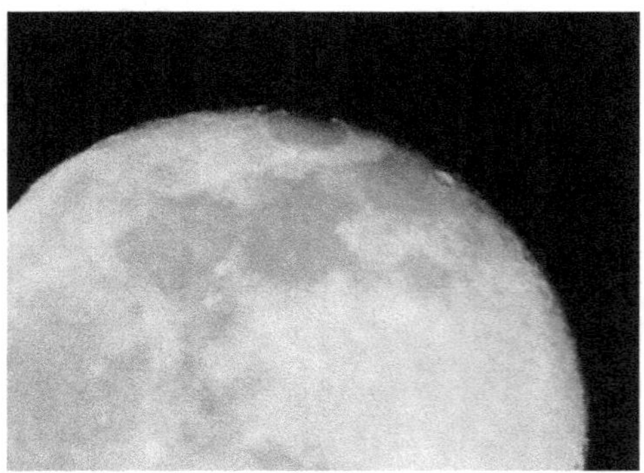

More than an emotion

Wherever you are I will be there
Especially when life doesn't treat you fair
Wherever you go I will follow you
No matter what you go through
Whatever you do I will support you
Where you are I will be there too
I will love you always and forever
You won't worry to lose me ever
My life is yours to share
For a love like this is so very rare.

Time.2

Each step forward little by little
It might seem to some a slight bit fickle
Moving but a moment
Part of every component
It holds all things
And with it, it brings
All of the memories
The rewards and the fees
You cannot steal it
But you certainly feel it
Always the same, but still a bit different
It causes all things magnificent
For if it were to not be
There would be nothing left to see
It would be end of all things
An emptiness would ring
Everything that is to be
Would never come to be seen

The red fox

The red fox is leading you, on and on you go
You can't stop to think, you don't even know
Where, when or how it came to be
There's not much to be sure of, can't even trust what you
see
Keep following the red fox, on and on you go
The sights are getting twisted yet nothing to show
Hear the piercing noises, the sky is red, black and blue
Keep on going downward, it's everything but new
Stay after that red fox, on and on you go
The lines are getting blurred now, whether friend or foe
It's hard to say which way's the right one
Finding nothing, ever on the run
Looks like the red fox got you, on and on no more
Next time don't trust the red fox, or else you'll hit the floor.

My Puddle

When I look into this puddle
I see a mighty muddle
Of all the things confusing
Both boring and amusing
It isn't until after
When I look a little farther
That I see this great big puddle
Will no longer my mind confuddle.

One Day

You are one of the greatest I know
You brighten each day anywhere you go
I forgive myself not for missing a moment with you
If only back then, in present and future you knew
Just what the greatest I see you to be
If only then and always you chose to be with me
I crown you forever my one true love
Perhaps with the magic of all the stars up above
I will have you one day, to make mine true
And together begin our chapter anew.

Positive, Pass it on

To a lady I once knew
Who shared with me a point of view
Something that is so kind
I certainly do not mind
To pass on the perspective
Of something corrective
To so many behaviours
And lend out a favour
To someone in need
That will in turn lead
To the flow of the good
And make the world as it should
Through nothing more than small actions
Inching forward each day just by a fraction.

My Buddy Darren

For a buddy of mine
Who said to me one time
If only I had the brain
I have now without the pain
When I had the energy before
I would have accomplished so much more
Well for you my friend
Life seems to lend
The rough patches come
But you knew when to run
Toward a different direction
And take upon your reflection
To start a new road
A leave behind the bad load
Of you I am so proud
To see it clear and loud
You are one of the good ones
And I love you fully tons!

Take it on

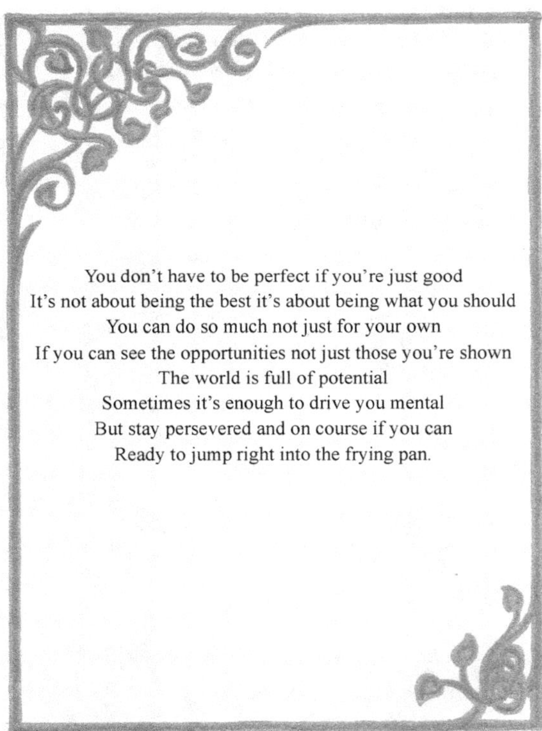

You don't have to be perfect if you're just good
It's not about being the best it's about being what you should
You can do so much not just for your own
If you can see the opportunities not just those you're shown
The world is full of potential
Sometimes it's enough to drive you mental
But stay persevered and on course if you can
Ready to jump right into the frying pan.

Everyday

This day is glorious if just because
And I feel like I just can't get enough
The air is fresh and the grass is green
Which is enough to find the happy in me
Even if the world throws rubbish at you
Know that there's always a way to get through
It's never the end unless you give in
Look for the signs hidden within
The sun on your skin
Or a word from your kin
Will help you find the power
To shelter your heart, even in the showers.

To My Love

I just wanted to let you know
You make each of my days glow
Full of happiness and total love
Your soul fits mine just like a glove
Forever I want to be by your side
Together through life we shall ride
We might have slightly missed before
But it just makes me want you more
I will wait as long as I have to
Even if our days are just a few
I can't wait to hold you in my arms
To keep your heart safe, with all of my charms.

A World Like This

With the world so beautiful
It's only fitting that I knew
Of the wonders to be seen
And the journey and what it means
Every big thing and the small
Sometimes I feel like a fool
Just to think about an action so common
Like the simple production of pollen
And just how amazing this planet really is
How we should appreciate all of this
The sky and all its wonders
The river and how it thunders
All the different butterflies
100s of them and that's no lie
These things are all around us
Sometimes you might think, what's the fuss
But appreciate what's there
Even down to the pear
That's grows on the tree
From nothing more than a seed
To the greatest of features
Far out of most reaches
Like the pools of molten rock
Which to see is a bit of a shock
As it pours out the ground
In rivers of sound
And hot piercing heat
One of nature's amazing feats
Cause there's so much to see
You don't need to be
Anything special
To not have to settle

Just look around you
There's more than just a few
Reasons to smile
That've been there all the while.

What's the race?

It's a pleasure to show
What few people know
About the things that matter
Through which boundaries may shatter
That life is more than this
So much so most will miss
The things that are important
Some will find even discordant
But believe it is there
With the notion to share
So we don't just survive
But start to truly thrive.

Choice Words

I don't know quite how to convey
Exactly what it is that I want to say
But maybe a few choice words
In the form of a rhyme just might be heard
By you for what it is I have to share
I always have and always will care
About you the most
For you are the host
Of my heart true and pure
Of this I am sure
And I don't want to wait
Or leave it up to the fates
To spend a life with you
And create an adventure anew.

Wondrous Day

Weaving on your wondrous way
Through this marvellous day
If it isn't for a minute
You don't push to your limit
You'll never get the best out of the day.

Home Vol. 1

The raindrops they'd patter on the roof as they fall
Hearing the wind whip through the trees standing tall
The tiles they'd batter on the beams up above
The spiders retreat into their webs like a glove
Wrapped up in layers, everyone took brace
To see through this weather hopefully post haste
The cold set in it chills to the bone
It's funny to think this place we called home
For one it has been a fortress of change
Sometimes it has been just anguish and pained
For it was only meant to be
A brief moment in our history
But so life had it it has become
A place to get more than one thing done
A whole bunch of memories
Trials and serenities
To look back when needed
And see what we've succeeded.

Poison

It's curious to me
This thing that I see
It befuddles my eye
I ask myself why
Could it be such a thing
That is only a kin
To others that grow
But little do we know
About these wee creatures
That have all these strange features
And it confuses me still
How that they will
Continue to thrive
In a world as it dies
If we do not stop
The chaos and rot
Pouring into the ground
'til it comes back around
And floods the oceans
Without even the notion
That if we continue
We might miss our window
To change the course
Of this sheer human force.

Climbing to the top

Why is it so hard to keep on this way
Why is it no matter they never seem to say
That you're doing a good enough job
That you're making enough bob
That life is good and will be well
All I want is to hear the bell
The signal I have reached the top
With everything not a flop
Where hard work pays
And so long to the days
That hang in the shadow
Of the failures of my days harrow
Where things have a lining
Of bright silvery shining
And my days are no longer numbered
For the future is not encumbered
With the darkness or regret
Then I'll wager a bet
On myself at last
And leave dust on the past.

A poem to make you smile

Whenever you feel low
From me you should know
You are one of the best things to be
When you walk into the room
It changes my tune
My happy meter goes through the roof
It makes my day brighter
And my heart feels lighter
I just want to hold you close
Your presence is a blessing
I'm not even messing
It's the single greatest thing to happen
You're one of the best
Unlike so many of the rest
You're always my reason and fair
You don't always feel it
But no one can steal it
It goes right through to your core
Cause your worth more than you credit
It's not about the after-play edit
You're genuinely the best one there is
I'll help you to juggle
Your trials and your troubles
If only you'll let me be there
And when you need a moment
I'll be your missing component
And everything will be brighter therefore

For my Fool

You are the friend of mine, who in my heart forever stays
The one constant who's friendship always pays
To keep you close to me to through the good and the bad
You'll always be there for me even when everyone else
thinks I'm mad!
I love everything about you, you are the absolute best
For me personally a little bit better than all the rest
Even when there's distance between us I know you're
always there
That you will always be there and forever you will care
Please know that the feeling is mutual, you will always
have me
I am yours to call on whatever you might need

Waiting

To the little one who wants to be
Who as of now I've yet to see
It's just the thought of you
I know one day will be true
For you are loved before you begin
The want of your life more than a whim
One day you'll be here and you will see
Just how much your mummy wants you to be
Here in this world to love and to laugh
To make your decisions and carve your own path
I will always love you and be here to protect you
I know one day you'll be here to love me too.

Society dictates

Trying to find the quiet, a moment in the mayhem
So much on your mind, just try to save them
It seems never ending, all these dates and numbers
Always on the go, even when most slumber
It's not a performance practice it isn't a chance luck draw
They will always be there of that you can certainly be sure
It feels like treading water, there's no rest in sight
To get ahead it just can't happen, try as you might
One will hit you then the next, over again it just won't stop
No time to cry it won't help, summon the energy no time to
flop
It's an eternal process you've just got to get on board
It all comes down to you, it's that or get floored.

One Wrong Move

Playing with this fire, waiting to get burnt
You know it's wrong, but you haven't learnt
Run with adrenaline keep on pacing
Time it is futile ever it is wasting
Jumping through hoops
Sending you through loops
Throwing oil as it burns
Watching the ember as it turns
Into a blaze
That leaves everything in haze
Of smog and confusion
A full head spin of illusion
You're playing with fire just waiting to get burnt.

Here

You can move mountains if only you believe it
Knowledge is there you've just got to retrieve it
Nothing will stop you if your mind is open
Now you are here and your heart is awoken
There's so much to do if only you see
What can be accomplished and what could yet be
Not holding back, that's a loser's game
You're destined for greater, not just safe and plain.

Missing Piece

When you've lost that someone, that reason to be
You don't know how to function, you can't even see
Every moment feels a lifetime, when your muse is not here
The heartache matched only by the loneliness and fear
What the future holds without them, you can't even fathom
The thought of the space left throws your heart into spasm
Each moment awake whilst your dearest is sleeping
Is a chance to give honour and thanks for your first meeting
To take each step of the rest of your life
As they would have wanted, despite the strife
You live now for them, how they would have dreamed it
And little by little it will actually be it
Cause they will be there, in every last drop
Just willing you on and never to stop.

Four walls

The walk of life is like the edge of a knife
Just take a slice and roll the dice
Shatter these skies and these brilliant lies
Forever is a moment in the large scale component
The human race is destined to taste
Bitter til the end until we all descend
The chances we take are likely to break
But persistence is key if you want to live free
From the irons and the chains that suffocate our brains
Each beat of your heart is a treat from the start
Use it for great things, hear how your heart sings
Cause it's not often the first thought despite what you've been taught
You wonder a many if your last pound and penny
Is enough to see you through and reach a day of new
The wishes and dreams if ever they seemed
A far distant cry from what's in front of my eye
But blessed it seems is the life I've been deemed
Do it all justice for those who don't trust us
And be the one standing, tall strong and demanding
From flight it will tell if this is all but a cell
Of my own mind's creation just bursting with expectation.

Bring me to you

These things they say
Meaning something it may
I could quite well do
With a sign or two
To find my way
Out of this grey
And into the blue
And bring me to you.

These dreams

To jump through the skies
Soaring high above the lies
On these moonlit nights
The dreams take flight
Making their own way
Through the dark days
Never holding back
Here you'll find no lack
Of adventure and heart
These dark skies start
With just a small thought
Enough to get caught
Up in the mind
So you can then find
A hero one day
Or a demon to slay
True love to find
No heart to mind
Once in a lifetime
Every single nighttime.

Come find me

Come find me on exploding star
We'll meet alone come distance far
No space no time
Shows our fault line
If once it's a moment to be.

No doubt

To find out what it all means
Do not be afraid to dream
You're nothing without
Aspirations no doubt
There's so much out there to be seen.

There is always something

Ignition of this magic
Is the only way to have it
Believe in the beauty
No need to be snooty
There's much to discover
One mystery then another
This world is divine
If you spend the time
To open your eyes
To the wonder that lies
Throughout this great place
Like sharing and grace
So stunning is the land
That grows with us hand in hand
So treasured it should be
All the things there are to see
The days and the nights
The great urban lights
These feats of nature and man
To be seen just as it can
Take a minute all around you
There will be more than a few
Places to fit in this tight web knit.

Step by Step

Onward upward forward you go
Each step further more to show
Willing the distance
Determination persistence
Each step forward further you go

It's never forever

For you my friend, I write these words
To express a point quite like a nerd
For you have taught me many things
The thought of losing you totally stings
I'll take every minute of this life that you lived
And cherish it forever even the bits that you hid
Cause it all together makes you who you are to me
I love you for all of it when the real you I see.

This day

As the day grows close
The feelings seem most
Unbearable at first
But brings with it a thirst
For more from that day
Than first did I say
It's a pickle to figure
How this conundrum grows bigger
Emotions they may
Just get in the way
But the trouble it can't
Fix itself no it shan't
Perhaps the only way
Is to give into the play
See the chips fall
And wait for the call
Of what the fates make
I'll be ready to take.

From one to another

On the wings of a wish
Do fly a great gift
From one to another
Seemingly to discover
Wherein to find kind heart
From the end right to the start
Blessed are the tokens
Of kind all but misspoken
Gestures and dues
Apart from some views
Cross them in vain
Not worthy the strain
Define the right cause
To raise up the floors
Of judgement and value
On this day shall you?

Take thee

Wicked are the witches that run this great race
All powers willing to bring you from grace
Fear of the unknown won't bare you no favour
Hidden in the shadows is evil's true flavour
Face it in strength and with true instinct fight
For love lust or power just don't lose the sight
Piercing are the sirens as hells gates descend
Following through all things right up to end
Deluding is this gaze through all eyes but those
Taking the torment for that is what's been chose
Clouded in red smoke the fogs of despair
Putrid are the faces of those who weren't there
Dying are the angels over promises told
Barely there requiems for the heroes in the cold
Tainted run the waters that nourish this place
Threatening feelings that yet have no face
Patiently lurking in hollows that surround
Festering upward until hope it has found
Can't get out the motion of these things that be
Never it seems will this soul be free.

If there were no soldiers

Spots or stripes and all different styles
It's not about the face just count up the smiles
It doesn't matter the colour it's all one and the same
Its for something deeper that's where lies the blame
To be good of moral and stand up and say
If there were no soldiers how would the men play
Be less of the fighting put our attentions to good
Make the world stronger in unity we should
There still is the time to change up our fate
But things need to happen they just cannot wait
Troubles always stirring what is the point
Problems a plenty such tremendous disjoint
We're capable of more why waste the potential
Combine what we've got, this is essential.

You are amazing

You try as you might to be the best one
You do it all right and try to be fun
You set out your boundaries and keep the line
Your always upfront and give them the time
You do everything you can to never let them down
You always persist that no one sees your frown
You always are there to put things right
You carry it with you this beautiful light
You make people's lives brighter everyday
You've got a burden to carry in that sort of way
You make it look easy, this caring thing
You put everyone first despite the sting
You're a wonder to many and a treasure to the rest
You're a beautiful person, one of the best
Your problem is twofold, it's just bad luck
You are that amazing that's why you give a fuck
You feel for others and you can't say no
You ask yourself why cause it just goes to show
You can't do it all right all of the time
You're more than these moments, just listen to this rhyme
You've nothing to regret it'll work out best
You couldn't be another way else you'd be like all the rest
You're everything to me so don't doubt yourself
You'll always have this to keep on the shelf
I'll love you forever, you'll always have me
I'll be there for you whatever you need.

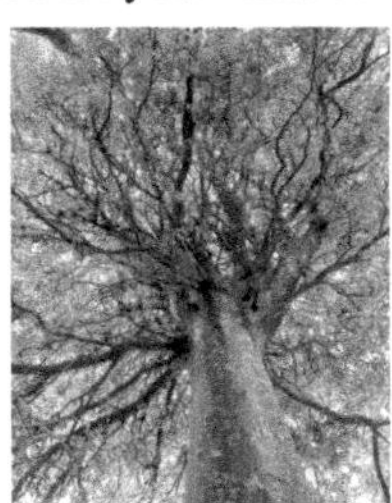

Our Secret Place

The place in which we can just be
A bubble of sorts, only we can see
The best of all worlds yours and mine
That of which no one else can find
The beauty of this place is it's just you and me
Ever that way, I'd like it to be
This place is peaceful it's good for the soul
Everything else, has a way of taking its toll
Love is in this place, quite like no other
From all things hateful we will take cover
My place is your place this is for us
Never to end pass by all the fuss
This is our place in which I can shield you
From everything wrong and miserable too
I will protect you no harm will come
I will be there with you each new sun
This place is our place forever it is
You and I together in eternal bliss.

www.ingramcontent.com/pod-product-compliance
Lightning Source LLC
LaVergne TN
LVHW041226200726
843507LV00013B/2596